The Story of a Special Day
Volume 1

January

1

January 1 is the first day of the year. There are 364 days remaining (336 in leap years) until the end of the year.

by Michael Dobson

Timespinner
Press

This book is also available in e-book form for Kindle, e-pub devices, and other formats from your favorite online booksellers.

For more information about the series, about us, or about your special day, please email us at editor@timespinnerpress.com.

Look for other volumes in *The Story of a Special Day*, coming often. See www.timespinnerpress.com for details and for the most recent information.

Table of Contents

For the definition of "O.S.," "N.S.," "CE," and "BCE" used with some dates , see the section "On Names and Dates."

Cover: New Year's Eve fireworks in Tyrol, Austria. (Photo: Ximeg, CC BY-SA 3.0) — for the EVENT OF THE DAY.

Quote of the Day

"How can I tell what I think till I see what I say?"

E. M. Forster, novelist
born January 1, 1879

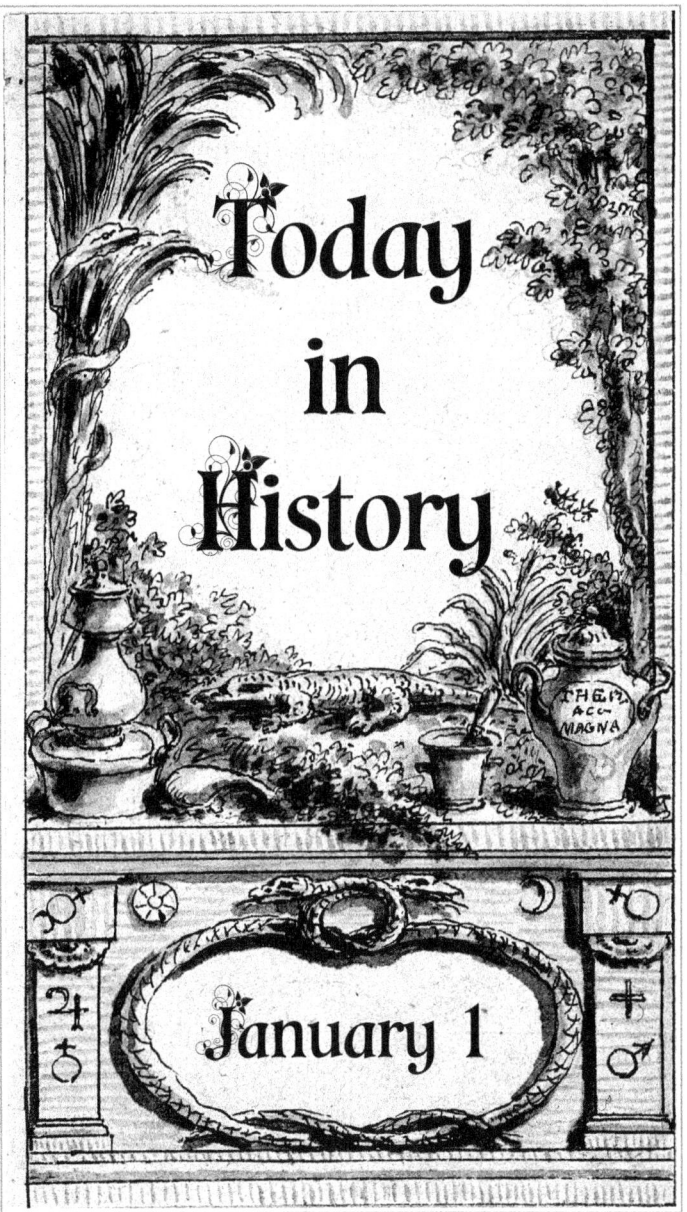

Today in History

January 1

A 1910 New Year's Day postcard

Event of the Day
The New Year Begins!

For most of the world, the New Year begins on January 1, making New Year's Day the most celebrated public holiday around the world.

New Year's Day officially begins at midnight, so most New Year's Eve parties and celebrations begin in one year and end in the next. Major fireworks displays can be seen in many cities. The famous Times Square countdown in New York City attracts huge crowds and millions more on television.

In some cultures the festivities go on until the next day; in others New Year's Day is more about relaxing and watching TV. In the United States, the Rose Bowl (and accompanying parade) and the Orange Bowl college football games are big television draws. The National Hockey League's Winter Classic and association football (soccer) games in Europe are all part of New Year's Day for millions around the world.

For the brave and hardy in colder climes, New Year's Day is the occasion for a Polar Bear Plunge, diving into ice cold water to raise money for charity or just for fun!

New Year's Day Around the World

In the **Bahamas**, New Year's Day is the occasion for the annual Junkanoo parade. In the **Philippines,** people set off firecrackers and blow horns to dispel evil spirits.

In **Greece** and **Cyprus**, families switch off their lights at midnight and slice the *vassilopita*. One of the slices contains a coin, and whoever gets the coin will have good luck all year long. The **Spanish** keep twelve grapes on hand for when the clock strikes midnight. For good luck all year long, eat them all before the chimes of the clock finish striking twelve.

The **Scots** celebrate *Hogmanay,* the last day of the year, with the singing of Auld Lang Syne at midnight. Although that custom originated in Scotland, it has become traditional in many other countries. The **Welsh** hold *Calennig* celebrations, with gift giving traditional on New Year's morning.

Because religion was suppressed in the **former Soviet Union**, New Year's Day (*Novy God*, or Новый Год), has become a sort of stand-in Christmas, with Christmas trees and a Grandfather Frost who brings presents to children.

The same phrase, *Novy God* (נובי גוד) also means New Year's Day in **Israel**, celebrated primarily by first- or second-generation Russian immigrants. Israelis also celebrate New Year's Eve as *Sylvester*. **Jewish New Year's Day**, *Rosh Hashanah*, falls sometime in September or October.

Orthodox, Anglican, and Lutheran churches celebrate the Feast of the Circumcision of Christ on January 1, because under Hebrew tradition this ritual would have taken place on the eighth day following his birth on December 25. **Catholics** celebrate the Solemnity of Mary, Mother of God, a Holy Day of Obligation.

Happy New Year postcard by Frances Brundage (1910)

How New Year's Day Became January 1

January 1 wasn't always New Year's Day. From ancient Mesopotamia through the early days of Rome, March was considered the beginning of the new year. The very first known January 1 New Years celebration dates back to 153 BCE!

In 46 BCE, Julius Caesar made a major calendar reform, and his Julian calendar would last for nearly 1,500 years. However, the official day of the new year

A French New Year's card wishing "Bonne année" with a
champagne toast

wasn't standardized. At different times and in
different countries, December 25, March 1, March 25,
and Easter were all used.

The modern Gregorian calendar*, used today by
most of the world, standardized January 1 as the first
day of the new year. Even though the calendar was
issued in 1582, it took hundreds of years for it to
become standard. Great Britain (and its North
American colonies) didn't adopt the Gregorian
calendar (and a January 1 New Year) until 1752!

---

* What is a Gregorian calendar? How does it differ from other
calendars? For details, see "What Day of the Week is January 1?"

New Year's Celebrations in Other Calendars

Some countries don't use the Gregorian calendar or use a different calendar for some purposes, often religious. Many **Orthodox Christian** denominations, for example, use the older Julian calendar for liturgical purposes. January 1 on the Julian calendar falls on the Gregorian January 13, so January 13 is celebrated as New Year's Day some places.

In **Cambodian** and **Thailand,** New Year's Day falls either on April 13 or 14. In **Ethiopia**, New Year's Day is known as *Enkutatash*, and is celebrated on September 11 (September 12 in leap years).

Chinese New Year falls on the first day of the lunar calendar, which can be any day between January 20 and February 20. The **Vietnamese** celebrate *Têt* on the same day. Although **Koreans** celebrate January 1, they also celebrate the first day of the lunar calendar as *Seollal* (설날).

The **Islamic world** uses a lunar calendar, which means that *Ras as-Sanah al-Hijriyah* (رأس السنة الهجرية), which takes place on the first day of Muharram, occurs on a different Gregorian day each year.

Iranians, Central Asians, and others celebrate *Nowruz*, the first day of spring and the beginning of the year in the traditional Iranian calendar. It takes place most often on March 21, but can sometimes take place on the previous or following day. It is of Zoroastrian origin.

On the **Indian subcontinent**, the **Marwari** New Year is celebrated on the first day of *Diwali*, the

Hindu festival of lights and a major celebration. The **Gujarati** celebrate the next day as New Year's, and the **Nepalese** the fourth day afterward. Diwali occurs sometime from mid-October to mid-November. **Bengalis** and others celebrate when the Sun enters Aries on the Hindu calendar, normally April 14 or 15. **Sikhs** celebrate on March 14.

No matter when or how you celebrate, the transition from the old year to the new one is an important moment in every culture.

Happy New Year!

Father Time (from *Slings and Arrows*, Edwin Edgett, 1922)

An Italian immigrant at Ellis Island. The Ellis Island immigration center opened January 1, 1890. (Photo: Lewis Wickes Hine, courtesy Los Angeles County Museum of Art)

What Happened on January 1?

From the creation of great works of engineering and art, to devastating wars and natural disasters, thousands of years of history have left their mark on each and every day of the year. Here are some important events that occurred on January 1. (Items with a photo or illustration are boxed.)

1772 — The first **traveler's checks** are issued by the London Credit Exchange Company. They could be used in 90 European cities.

1773 — The hymn **"Amazing Grace"** is sung in a prayer meeting for the first time.

1781 — During the American Revolutionary War, a mutiny of soldiers in the Continental Army begins. Known as the **Pennsylvania Line mutiny,** it ended eight days later with a settlement for the rebelling soldiers.

1801 — The merger of the kingdoms of Great Britain and Ireland creates the **United Kingdom** of Great Britain and Ireland (today, Northern Ireland).

1804 — **Haiti declares independence from France,** becoming the first black republic and second independent nation in North America.

1808 — The **United States outlaws the importation of slaves.** Slaves already in the United States are not affected.

1863 — The **Emancipation Proclamation,** an executive order issued by President Abraham Lincoln, officially frees slaves in the Confederate states.

"First Reading of the Emancipation Proclamation of Abraham Lincoln," by Francis Bicknell Carpenter (1864)

1890 — The **Ellis Island** Immigration Station, located on a small island in the New York Bay, opens. By the time it closes in 1954, over twelve million immigrants will pass through its doors. *(Photo page 8)*

1898 — New York City annexes the East Bronx, Brooklyn, most of Queens County, and Staten Island, creating **Greater New York City.**

1902 — The **first college football bowl game**, the Rose Bowl, is played in Pasadena, California, between Michigan and Stanford.

1908 — A ball is dropped in New York City's **Times Square** to mark the start of the New Year, creating an annual tradition.

1912 — The **Republic of China is formed**, and rules mainland China until it falls to the People's Republic of China in 1949.

1934 — **Alcatraz** Island becomes a US Federal prison.

Alcatraz (Photo: Jon Sullivan)

1954 — The first **coast-to-coast broadcast** in the US takes place, the Tournament of Roses on NBC. Because color televisions were not yet available, public demonstrations on prototypes were given around the country.

1959 — **Fidel Castro's** forces oust the Batista government and take over the rule of Cuba.

1971 — **Cigarette advertising** is banned on American television.

1983 — The ARPANET data network adopts the TCP/IP protocol, becoming the **Internet.**

1984 — The nationwide American Telephone & Telegraph Company **(AT&T) is broken up** into 22 companies, settling an antitrust suit by the US Department of Justice.

1988 — Three **Lutheran church bodies merge**, becoming the Evangelical Lutheran Church in America.

1993 — **Czechoslovakia is divided** into the Czech Republic and Slovakia.

1999 — The **Euro** is introduced.

The Euro sign outside the European Central Bank, Frankfurt,
Germany. (Photo: Lars Aronsson, CC BY-SA 1.0)

Quote of the Day

"I'm a kind of paranoiac in reverse. I suspect people of plotting to make me happy."

J. D. Salinger, author
born January 1, 1919

Births
and
Deaths

January 1

Paul Revere, by John Singleton Copley (1768). Paul Revere was born January 1, 1735

Notable January 1 People

With the current world population at about seven billion people, on average about 19 million people also celebrate their birthdays on January 1 — and that isn't counting millions and millions who came before! No matter when you were born, you share your birthday with many special people whose accomplishments (and occasionally embarrassments) have been noted as part of history.

In this section, you'll meet fascinating people who share your birthday. They're organized by what they're famous for, and then in reverse chronological order from most recent to earliest. Those who are shown in photographs or artwork have a box around them. We don't have photos of everyone, so please forgive us if your favorite person is missing.

Some of these people you've heard of, others will be new to you, but they all make up an important part of the reason that January 1 is a truly special day!

Alfred Stieglitz in 1886 (self-portrait)

Who Was Born on January 1?

Art and Photography

Jerry Robinson, co-created Robin and the Joker for the *Batman* line of comics, member of the Comic Book Hall of Fame. *(1922)*

Alfred Stieglitz, helped make photography an accepted art form, husband of painter Georgia O'Keefe. *(1864)*

Business and Finance

Christine Lagarde, first woman to become managing director of the International Monetary Fund. *(1956)*

Ronald Perelman, investor who became one of the richest people in the world as well as one of the largest philanthropic donors. *(1943)*

James Sinegal, co-founder and CEO of Costco. *(1936)*

Vernon L. Smith, received the 2002 Nobel Memorial Prize in Economic Sciences for his work in experimental economic theory. *(1927)*

Espionage and Crime

Kim Philby, senior British intelligence officer who was a double agent for the Soviet Union, considered one of the most effective spies of all time. *(1912)*

J. Edgar Hoover, legendary first director of the FBI. *(1895)*

J. Edgar Hoover (Photo: Marion S. Trikosko for *US News and World Report*, courtesy Library of Congress)

Admiral Wilhelm Canaris, headed the Abwehr, or German military intelligence, during the Nazi regime, involved in clandestine anti-Hitler actitivities, executed for high treason. *(1887)*

"Wild Bill" Donovan, headed the Office of Strategic Services, predecessor to the modern CIA, during World War II. *(1883)*

Government and Politics

Betsy Ross, seamstress credited with making the first American flag. *(1752)*

Betsy Ross Sewing the American Flag, by Jean Leon Gerome Ferris (Courtesy Library of Congress)

Lorenzo de' Medici the Magnificent, influential Renaissance leader and patron of the arts. *(1449)*

Journalism and Letters

Olivia Goldsmith, best known as the author of the 1992 novel (and subsequent film) *The First Wives Club. (1949)*

Alan Berg, outspoken talk radio host assassinated by white nationalists, inspired the films *Betrayed* and *Talk Radio. (1934)*

Larry L. King, playwright and journalist best known for his play (later film) *The Best Little Whorehouse in Texas. (1929)*

Ernest Tidyman, author and screenwriter who created the African-American detective John Shaft in a series of novels, and wrote the screenplay for the 1971 film *Shaft,* featuring the character. He received an Academy Award for his screenplay for *The French Connection. (1928)*

J. D. Salinger, reclusive author of *The Catcher in the Rye. (1919)*

Audrey Wurdeman, youngest winner of the Pulitzer Prize for Poetry, claimed to be the great-great-granddaughter of Percy Bysshe Shelley. *(1911)*

E. M. Forster, English novelist best known for such works as *Howard's End* and a *A Passage to India,* both made into films, nominated for the Nobel Prize in Literature sixteen times. *(1879)*

Sir James George Frazer, social anthropologist in mythology and comparative religion, author of the classic 1890 book *The Golden Bough. (1854)*

Military and Adventure

Abdul Ahad Momand (عبد الاحد مومند), first Afghani and fourth Muslim to travel into outer space. *(1959)*

John Garand, Canadian firearms designer who created the M1 Garand rifle used by US forces during World War II and the Korean War. *(1888)*

"Mad" Anthony Wayne, general during the American Revolutionary War, later served as General-in-Chief of the US Army. *(1745)*

Paul Revere, silversmith famous for alerting the colonial militia to the British advance prior to the battles of Lexington and Concord, immortalized in the Henry Wadsworth Longfellow 1861 poem "Paul Revere's Ride." *(1735 [O.S.† December 31, 1734]) (Photo page 16)*

Music

Grandmaster Flash, hip hop pioneer and leader of the Furious Five, first hip hop act ever inducted into the Rock and Roll Hall of Fame. *(1958)*

Milt Jackson, jazz vibraphonist during the bop era, best known as a member of the Modern Jazz Quartet. *(1923)*

---

† For the meaning of "O. S.," see "On Names and Dates."

Xavier Cugat, popular Latin bandleader who appeared in such films as *You Were Never Lovelier*, with Fred Astaire and Rita Hayworth. *(1900)*

Xavier Cugat

Performing Arts

Eden Riegel, won an Emmy for her role as Bianca Montgomery in the soap opera *All My Children.* *(1981)*

Verne Troyer, best known for playing "Mini-Me" in the *Austin Powers* film series. *(1969)*

Don Novello, comedian, writer, and actor best known for his portrayal of Father Guido Sarducci on the television series *Saturday Night Live.* *(1943)*

Frank Langella, stage and film actor nominated for an Academy Award for his role in the 2008 film *Frost/Nixon. (1938)*

Matt Robinson, actor best known as the first person to play Gordon on *Sesame Street. (1937)*

Matthew Beard, Jr., child actor best known for playing Stymie in the *Our Gang/Little Rascals* films. *(1925)*

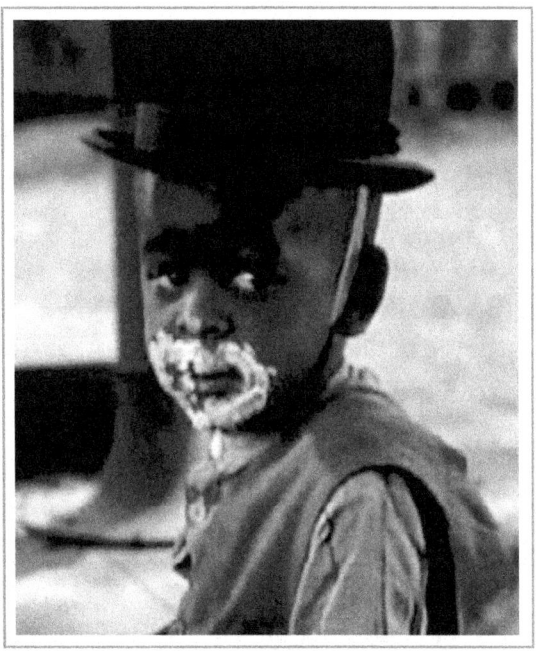

Matthew Beard Jr. as Stymie in *School's Out*

Dana Andrews, major movie star of the 1940s, best known for the 1946 film *The Best Years of Our Lives. (1909)*

William Fox, motion picture executive who founded the Fox Film Corporation, precursor of 20th Century Fox and the Fox TV network. *(1879)*

Religion

Huldrych Zwingli, Swiss leader in the Protestant Reformation. *(1484)*

Science and Technology

Sir Martin Evans, English biologist who shared the Nobel Prize in Physiology or Medicine for his research into the uses of embryonic stem cells. *(1941)*

Satyendra Nath Bose (সত্যেন্দ্রনাথ বসু), Bengali physicist important in the development of quantum mechanics, partnered with Albert Einstein to develop Bose-Einstein statistics and the theory of the Bose-Einstein condensate. The subatomic particles known as "bosons" are named for him. *(1894)*

Gustave Whitehead, pre-Wright Brothers aviation pioneer who claimed to be first to fly a powered aircraft. *(1874)*

Sports

Meryl Davis, ice dancer who won a gold medal in the 2014 Olympics, as well as the 18th season of *Dancing With the Stars. (1987)*

Gustave Whitehead (right, with daughter on his lap), along with members of his crew, with his 1901 monoplane

Derrick Thomas, linebaker for the Kansas City Chiefs, member of the Pro Football Hall of Fame. *(1967)*

Andrew Valmon, won two Olympic gold medals in the 4x400m relay. *(1965)*

Dave Silk, member of the Olympic gold medal winning 1980 US Men's hockey team that defeated the Soviet Union in the "Miracle on Ice." *(1958)*

Don Nehlen, college football coach for Bowling Green and West Virginia, member of the College Football Hall of Fame. *(1936)*

Jackie Parker, Canadian Football League player named to the College Football Hall of Fame and the Canadian Football Hall of Fame. *(1932)*

Doak Walker, Heisman Trophy winner and member of both the College and Pro Football Halls of Fame, namesake of the Doak Walker Award for the top running back in college football. *(1927)*

Rocky Graziano, world middleweight boxing champion whose autobiography *Somebody Up There Likes Me* became an Oscar-winning film. *(1919)*

"Hammerin'" Hank Greenberg, first baseman for the Detroit Tigers, considered one of the greatest sluggers of all time, first Jewish superstar in American team sports, member of the Baseball Hall of Fame. *(1911)*

Pierre de Coubertin, French educator and historian who founded the International Olympic Committee, considered the father of the modern Olympic Games. *(1863)*

Who Died on January 1?

Art and Photography

Edward Weston, influential American photographer who focused on people and places of the American West. *(1958)*

Government and Military

Mario Cuomo, governor of New York known for his speeches, called the "Hamlet on the Hudson" for his reluctance to seek the Democratic nomination for president in 1988 and 1992. *(2015)*

Claiborne Pell, US senator best known for sponsoring the Pell Grant financial aid program for American college students. *(2009)*

Shirley Chisholm, first African-American woman elected to the US Congress, first black candidate for a major party nomination for President of the United States. *(2005)*

Joe Foss, US Marine fighter ace and Medal of Honor winner in the Guadalcanal campaign, later governor of South Dakota. *(2003)*

James Francis Edward Stuart, known as the "Old Pretender," son of deposed English King James II and VII who unsuccessfully claimed the throne, father of Charles Edward Stuart, better known as "Bonnie Prince Charlie," or the "Young Pretender." *(1766)*

Journalism and Letters

William Wilfred Campbell, at one time considered the "unofficial poet laureate of Canada.". *(1918)*

Music and Dance

Patti Page, singer known for suhch hits as "Tennessee Waltz," "(How Much is That) Doggie in the Window?" and "Hush, Hush, Sweet Charlotte." *(2013)*

Hank Williams, influential country singer-songwriter whose most famous songs include "Your Cheatin' Heart," "Hey, Good Lookin'," and "I'm So Lonesome I Could Cry." *(1953)*

Johann Christian Bach, sometimes called "the English Bach" for his long residence in London; eleventh and youngest child of Johann Sebastian Bach. Known for his influence on the young Mozart. *(1782)*

Performing Arts

Donna Douglas, actress best known for playing Elly May on the sitcom *The Beverly Hillbillies. (2015)*

Juanita Moore, actress best known for her role as Annie Johnson in the 1959 film *Imitation of Life (2014)*

Hank Williams

Donna Douglas as Elly May Clampett

Ray Walston, actor best known for playing the title character on the TV sitcom *My Favorite Martian,* and as Judge Bone on *Picket Fences. (2001)*

Cesar Romero, actor best known for playing the Joker in the 1960s *Batman* television show. *(1994)*

Victor Buono, actor nominated for the Academy Award for his role in *Whatever Happened to Baby Jane?,* played villain King Tut on the 1960s *Batman* television show. *(1982)*

Maurice Chevalier, French actor and singer best known for his signature song, "Thank Heaven for Little Girls." *(1972)*

Maurice Chevalier

Barton MacLane, actor best known for playing General Peterson on the 1960s sitcom *I Dream of Jeannie. (1969)*

Margaret Sullivan, actress nominated for an Academy Award for the 1938 film *Three Comrades. (1960)*

Science and Technology

Eugene Wigner, Hungarian physicist who shared the 1963 Nobel Prize in Physics for his research into the atomic nucleus and elementary particles. *(1995)*

Admiral Grace Hopper, pioneering computer scientist who coined the phrase "debugging," based on actually removing a moth stuck in a relay, and with the famous adage, "It's easier to ask forgiveness than it is to get permission." *(1992)*

Grace Hopper (center) in front of the UNIVAC computer, circa 1960

Heinrich Hertz, German physicist who proved the existence of electromagnetic waves, namesake of the unit of radio frequency known as the "Hertz." *(1894)*

Martin Klaproth, chemist who discovered the elements uranium, zirconium, and cerium. *(1817)*

Sports

Helen Wills, called the "greatest female player in the history of tennis," member of the International Tennis Hall of Fame. *(1998)*

Helen Wills

Quote of the Day

"Old age isn't so bad when you consider the alternative."

Maurice Chevalier, singer and actor
died January 1, 1972

Holidays
Around
the World

January 1

USAF Tech. Sgt. Jennifer Myers demonstrates a Kwanzaa ritual
where she lights a candle in the Kinara.
(Photo: Christopher Myers, courtesy US Air Force)

Holidays Around the World

If you're looking for a reason to take your special day off, you should know that every single day is a holiday somewhere in the world! Here's some of what you can celebrate on January 1!

Kwanzaa — Day of Imani

A week-long festival honoring the African heritage in African-American culture, Kwanzaa is observed each year from December 26 until January 1. The name comes from the Swahili *matunda ya kwanza,* meaning "first fruits of the harvest."

Each of the seven days of Kwanzaa is devoted to a different core principle: *Umoja* (unity), *Kujichagulia* (self-determination), *Ujima* (collective work and responsibility), *Ujamaa* (cooperative economics), *Nia* (purpose), *Kuumba* (creativity), and on the last day, January 1, *Imani* (faith).

From its origins in the 1960s, Kwanzaa is now celebrated by millions of people, primarily in the US and Canada. Joyous Kwanzaa!

Christmas Season

Eighth Day and Night of Christmas

Ready for eight maids a'milking? For most Western Christian denominations, the "Twelvetide," or Twelve Days of Christmas (celebrated in the famous song), begins on Christmas Day (some begin the day after) and runs until January 5 or 6, making New Year's Day the eighth day of Christmas (seventh if you start the day after).

Eastern Orthodox Christians who keep to the old Julian‡ calendar celebrate Christmas on January 7 and the twelve days run through January 19. Various celebrations and religious rites take place during the twelve days, though these vary by denomination.

Song poster for "The Twelve Days of Christmas," by Xavier Romero-Frias

---

‡ What's a Julian calendar? See "What Day of the Week is January 1?

General Events

Constitution Day (Italy)

Many nations set aside a day to commemorate their constitutions, which provide the fundamental laws for their nation. Italy's constitution took effect January 1, 1948.

Euro Day (European Union)

The Euro, a common currency for the European Union, became legal tender on January 1, 1999.

Founding Day (Taiwan)

Taiwan commemorates the proclamation of the Republic of China on January 1, 1912.

Global Family Day (United States)

Arising from a United Nations millenium celebration called "One Day in Peace," Global Family Day urges "one day of peace and sharing" on January 1.

Independence Day (Brunei, Haiti, Sudan)

When a nation becomes independent or achieves statehood, there is often an annual commemoration of this momentous occasion.

Three nations celebrate Independence Day on January 1. The nation of Brunei received its independence from the United Kingdom on January 1, 1984. Haiti commemorates its declaration of independence from France on January 1, 1804. Finally, the Sudan celebrates its independence from Egypt and the United Kingdom on January 1, 1956.

Jump-Up Day (Montserrat)

The Caribbean nation of Montserrat commemorates the emancipation of slaves in that nation on January 1, which is also the last day of Carnival on the island.

Triunfo de la Revolución (Cuba)

Cuba celebrates the Triumph of the Revolution led by Fidel Castro as a public holiday each January 1.

Vėliavos diena (Lithuania)

Many nations set aside a day to honor their nation's flag. In Lithuania, "Flag's Day" commemorates the raising of the Lithuanian flag on Gediminas's Tower on January 1, 1919.

Food Holidays

Bloody Mary cocktail
(Photo: Tibuhero CC
BY-SA 4.0)

In the United States, almost every day of the year is dedicated to a particular food. (Some other countries also have official food days, but only in America is there one every single day!) Sponsored by manufacturers, retailers, farmers, or simply fans, these days are often proclaimed by the President, Congress, state governors, or mayors. Given that there are more different foods than days of the year, some days honor more than one kind of food!

In the US, January 1 is **National Bloody Mary Day.** Bloody mary cocktails are made with vodka, tomato juice, and a wide variety of spices, giving its reputation as "the world's most complex cocktail."

It gets its name from Queen Mary of England, who persecuted Protestants in the 16th century, though some claim it was named for movie star Mary Pickford. There is a widespread belief that drinking a bloody mary in the morning will relieve a hangover (presumably left over from New Year's Eve), Foodimentary informs us that while it might temporarily alleviate some of the symptoms, it will ultimately make things worse by dehydrating the drinker.

In addition, the entire month of January is used to celebrate numerous foods.

- California Dried Plum Digestive Health Month
- Fat Free Living Month
- National Hot Tea Month
- National Oatmeal Month
- National Slow Cooking Month
- National Soup Month
- National Baking Month
- National Fat Free Living Month

And while we're on the subject of food, January is also **Weight Loss Awareness Month**, so it's a good time to make (and keep) those New Year's resolutions!

Religious Celebrations

Christian saint days

Each day in the year is considered a feast day for one or more saints. They are somewhat different in western Christianity (Catholicism and many forms of Protestantism) and in eastern (Orthodox) Christianity. There are many others; this is a selection.

In *Western Christianity*, January 1 is the feast day of Saints Adalard of Corbie, Basil the Great, Fulgentius of Ruspe, Giuseppe Maria Tomasi, Telemachus, and Zygmunt Gorazdowski..

In *Eastern Orthodox Christianity*, it is also the commemoration of Saints Gregory of Nazianzus the Elder, Emilia, Theodosius of Tryglia, Eugendus, Fanchea of Killeany, Justin of Chieti, Felix of Bourges, Connat, Maelrhys, Clarus, Cúan, Peter of Atroa, William of Dijon, Peter Mogila, and Athanasius of Poltava. (These people are honored on December 19 by "Old Calendrists.")

Feast of the Circumcision of Christ

Under Hebrew religious law, the ritual circumcision of newborn is eight days after the birth, so the Circumcision of Christ is celebrated on January 1, eight days after Christmas.

This is also celebrated as the **Feast of the Holy Name of Jesus**, although that is sometimes celebrated on January 3. In Medieval times, particularly in France, January 1 was celebrated as the **Feast of Fools,** especially in France, but

widespread misbehavior under the "Lord of
Misrule" caused this celebration to be banned
officially in 1431, though some continuted to
celebrate it as late as 1644.

Kalpataru Diwas (Ramakrishna adherents)

Monks of the Ramakrishna Math order of Hinduism
commemorate January 1, 1886, as the date that 19th
century religious leader Ramakrishna proclaimed
himself an avatar, God incarnate on Earth.

Kamakura Ebisu (鎌倉えびす) (Shinto)

January 1 begins a three-day festival in the Japanese
city of Kamakura to celebrate Ebisu (恵比須), the god
of commerce and one of the seven gods of fortune. In
the festival, young women in traditional garb sell
lucky charms made of bamboo and sake.

Honorary Months

Presidents, Congresses, and nations around the
world issue proclamations recognizing particular
months to honor certain causes. These events
generally fall in January, though honorary months do
come and go. Holidays established by states and
nonprofit organizations are listed if verified. If not
otherwise specified, all months are US. There is some
variation from year to year; some celebratory months
get added and others get dropped. Two places to get
up to date information are the current edition of
Chase's Calendar of Events or the website
Brownielocks. Here are some honorary designations
for January.

- Adopt a Rescued Bird Month
- Bath Safety Month
- Be Kind to Food Servers Month
- Birth Defects Month
- California Dried Plum Digestive Month
- Cervical Health Awareness Month
- Financial Wellness Month
- Get Organized Month
- International Child-Centered Divorce Awareness Month
- International Creativity Month
- National Braille Literacy Month

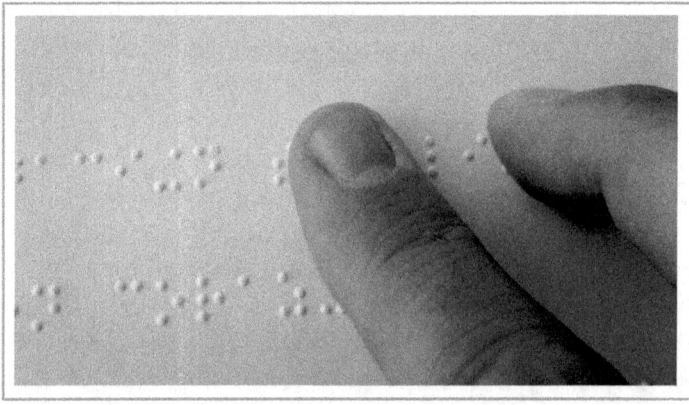

A person reading a braille book, for National Braille Literacy Month
(Photo: Antonio X Alonso CC BY-SA 2.0)

- National Clean Up Your Computer Month
- National Codependency Awareness Month
- National Mentoring Month

- National Polka Music Month
- National Poverty in America Awareness Month
- National Skating Month
- National Thank You Month
- National Volunteer Blood Donor Month
- Slavery and Human Trafficking Prevention Month
- Stalking Awareness Month
- Teen Driving Awareness Month
- Train Your Dog Month (also Walk Your Dog Month)

Moveable and Multi-Day Events

Some events take place over a specific week or time period. Start and finish dates may vary from year to year. Some events occur on different days each year (such as "fourth Saturday of a month"). These events sometimes take place on or include January 7.

First Week of January
- Celebration of Life Week
- Diet Resolution Week
- Silent Record Week
- New Year's Resolution Week

Week Long Celebrations that Sometimes Include January 1
- Home Office Safety and Security Week
- National Lose Weight/Feel Great Week

1st Friday (can be any day between January 1-7)

- Children's Day (Bahamas)

1st Monday (can be any day between January 1-7)

- Handsel Monday (Scotland and northern England)

Just For Fun

Anyone can make up a holiday, and many people do! These holidays are unofficial, and some of them come and go, but here are a few more reasons to celebrate on January 1!

- Ellis Island Day
- First Foot Day
- World Day of Peace
- Z Day

January, by Eugène Grasset

Quote of the Day

"It's easy to kill a movie. Just move it to January."

Mike Myers, as "Dr. Evil"
from the *Austin Powers* movies

About
the
Month
of

January

"January," from the *Brevarium Grimani* by Simon Bening (c.1510)

January: The First Month

That blasts of January
Would blow you through and through.
— *William Shakespeare,* The Winter's Tale

January wasn't always the first month in the year. In ancient Rome, March was the first month until about 450 BCE. Even after January became the official first month in the calendar, Romans still counted dates from the inauguration of the consuls, March 15 and May 1.

In the Middle Ages, Christian feast days were used to start the new year, including March 25 and December 25. It wasn't until the 16th century that European nations made January 1 the official start of the new year. (This was called "Circumcision Style" because January 1 was also celebrated as the Feast of the Circumcision of Jesus.)

The name January (*Ianuarius*) is derived from the Roman god Janus, the god of beginning and transitions. Janus gives his name to the Latin word for door (*ianua*), because January is the door to the year. Janus is normally portrayed as having two faces, one looking toward the future and one toward the past. In spite of that, the goddess Juno was the patron of that month.

In both the Julian and Gregorian calendars§, January is the first month of the year and one of seven months with 31 days. In the Northern Hemisphere, January is the coldest month of the year, and in the Southern Hemisphere, it's the warmest, equivalent to the Northern Hemisphere's July.

January in Other Cultures

The month of January has different names in different languages. Some nations use calendars other than the Gregorian, and their months may overlap with January. In lunar-based calendars, such as the Islamic calendar, months move through the seasons. Still, many languages often have a word for January itself.

Albanian: Janar

Anglo-Saxon: Wulf-monath

Arabic (Egypt, Sudan, Yemen): يونأغيناير (*yanāyir*)

Arabic (Levant): حزيركانون الثاني (*kānūn al-thānī*)

Arabic (Libya): الصهنار (*aynu n-nār*)

Arabic (Algeria and Tunisia): جأينجانفي (*Jānfī*)

Arabic (Morocco): غيناير (*yanāyər*)

Azerbaijani: Yanvar

Basque: Urtarril

Bulgarian: януари (*januari*)

---

§ To learn more about the different calendar types, see "What Day of the Week is January 7?"

Chinese: 一月 (Cantonese: *yātyuht*; Mandarin: *yīyuè*; Taiwanese: *it-goeh*)

Corsican: Ghjennaghju

Croatian: Siječanj

Czech: Leden

Finnish: Tammikuu (oak moon)

French: Janvier

German/Danish/Norwegian/Slovenian: Januar

Greek: Ιανουάριος (*Ianouários*)

Haitian Creole: Janvye

Hebrew: ינואר (*yanû'ar*)

Hindi: जनवरी (*janvarī*)

Hungarian: Január

Irish (Gaelic): Eanáir mí Eanáir

Italian: Gennaio

Japanese: 一月 (*ichigatsu*), 睦月 (*mutsuki*)

Kazakh: Қаңтар (*Ķaņtar*)

Korean: 일월 (*ilweol*)

Lithuanian: Sausis

Maori: Kohitātea

Old English: Se æfterra Gēola

Polish: Styczeń

Portuguese: Janeiro

Russian: январь (*janvar'*)

Scottish Gaelic: am Faoilleach

Sesotho: Pherekgong

Slovene: Prosinec

Spanish: Enero

Swahili/Dutch/Swedish: Januari
Swazi: Bhimbidvwane
Thai: มกราคม (*makarakhom*)
Turkish: Ocak
Vietnamese: 腩叉 (*tháng một*)
Walloon: Djanvî
Welsh: Ionawr
Yiddish: אייגויאַנואַר (*yanuar*)
Zulu: uJanuwari

Mengapa? Zašto?
Por quê? Чаму? 为什么呢？
Poukisa? كيون؟ Per què? Чому?
Tại sao? Miks?
Bakit? Kial? למה?
Waarom? Hvers vegna?
どうして？ פֿאַרװאָס? Niyə?
Warum? Dlaczego? Pourquoi?
ԻՆչու? Зашто? چرا؟ Quid?
Cén fáth? რატომ? Pam?
Zergatik? Proč? Miért?
Kwa nini? Hoekom? क्यों?
De ce? Kodėl?
เพราะเหตุใด Защо? Why?
Perché? Miksi?
لماذا؟ Prečo? Varför?
Γιατί;
Għaliex? ¿Por qué? Pse?
왜? Почему? Зошто?
Kāpēc? Neden?
Hvorfor? 為什麼呢？

January Sayings and Superstitions

Here are some sayings and superstitions associated with the month of January.

New Year Superstitions

- It's important to kiss those dearest to us at the stroke of the New Year to keep their affections for the next twelve months.

- The new year must not be seen with bare cupboards. Stock up on supplies and make sure there's plenty of money in ever wallet in the home.

- Do not begin the new year with the household in debt.

- The first person to enter your home after the stroke of midnight will tell you the kind of year you will have.

- Do not let anything leave your house on the first day of the year, not even garbage.

- Start your year off with good luck by eating hoppin' john, a dish made with black-eyed peas and rice (southern United States).

- Wear something new on January 1.

- Be sure to open the door at midnight to let the old year escape.

- Babies born on New Year's Day will always have good luck.

January Wedding Superstitions

- A January bride will be a prudent housekeeper, and very good tempered.

- Married in January's hoar and rime / Widowed you'll be before your prime.

- Married when the year is new, he'll be loving, kind and true.

January Symbols

Birthstone: Garnet, representing constancy.

Soviet postage stamp showing a geologist finding garnets

Birth Flower (Britain): Carnation, representing love, fascination, and distinction

Vase with Red and White Carnation on a Yellow Background, by Vincent van Gogh

Birth Flower (America): Carnation or Snowdrop (*Galanthus*)

A New Year's greeting card with snowdrops

Birth Flower (China): Plum blossom (*prunus mume*)

Red Plum Blossom (Photo: Frank Gualtieri)

Birth Flower (Japan): Camellia

Camellias (Clara Maria Pope)

Michael Dobson

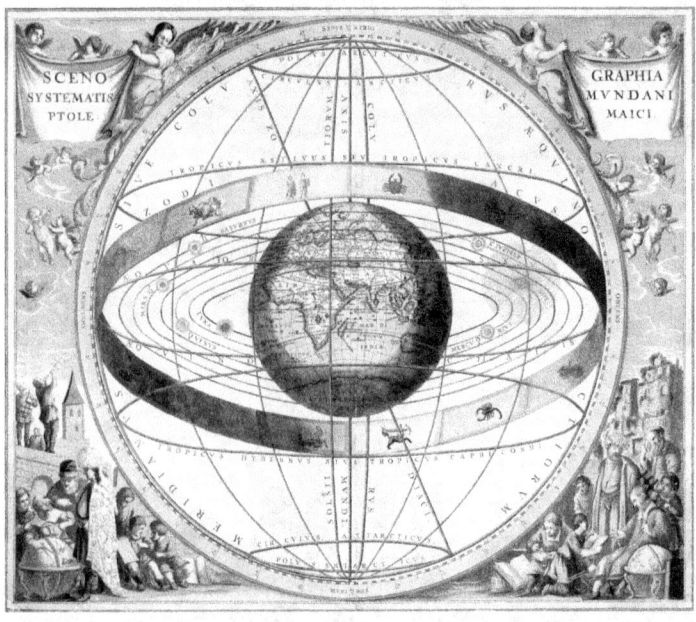

Scenography of the Ptolemaic Cosmography, by Johannes van
Loon, based on Andreas Cellarius's *Harmonia Macrocosmica*, 1660

January 1 Zodiac Signs

From the perspective of someone on Earth, the Sun appears to move through the sky throughout the year, along a path astronomers call the *ecliptic plane*. The ecliptic plane is divided into twelve constellations, known as the zodiac, based on traditionally observed patterns of stars. On your birthday, you can't see your constellation, because it's in the daytime sky.

The zodiac was first developed by Babylonian astronomers about 2,500 years ago. Because they were unaware that the Earth wobbles like a spinning top (known as *precession*), they didn't make allowance for the fact that the Sun's path through the zodiac changes over time.

That means there are now two sets of dates for your birth sign. The *tropical dates* are the original Babylonian dates; the *sidereal dates* tell you where the Sun actually appears as it moves along its annual path.

For January 1, the tropical signs is **Capricorn** and the sidereal sign is **Sagittarius**.

Capricorn

Tropical December 22 to January 20
Sidereal January 15 to February 14

The origins of the constellation Capricorn date back
to Sumeria and Babylonia. Based on Enki, the
Sumerian god of wisdom and waters, Capricorn has
the head and upper body of a mountain goat and the
lower body and tail of a fish. The mountain goat
represents ambition and intelligence, the fish
represents passion and spirituality.

An earth sign, Capricorn is ruled by the planet
Saturn. They are often thought to be responsible,
patient, ambitious and loyal, but can sometimes be
seen as conceited, distrusting, and unimaginative.
Capricornians are supposed to be compatible with
Taurus, Pisces, and Virgo, but not with Aries,
Sagittarius, or Leo.

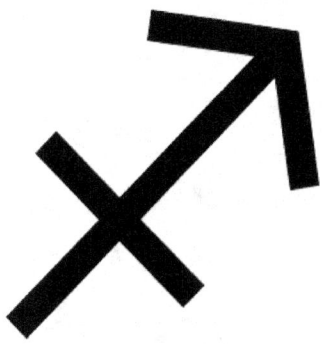

Sagittarius

Tropical November 23 to December 21
Sidereal December 16 to January 14

The centaur (half-man, half-horse) Chiron was famous as a healer and as an archer. He tutored Achilles, Jason (of Argonaut fame), and Hercules. Unfortunately for Chiron, Hercules accidentally shot him with an arrow that had been dipped in hydra poison. He was unable to find a cure, so gave up his immortality to free Prometheus, and died. In recognition of his sacrifice, Zeus placed him among the stars.

In astrology, Sagittarians are known for their independence and craving for adventure and excitement. They are encouraging and kind, but sometimes lack commitment. They are supposed to be compatible with Aries, Leo, and Libra, but not with Taurus, Scorpio, or Capricorn.

Illustration by Edward Penfield

What Day of the Week is January 1?

On what day of the week does January 1 fall?

Surprisingly, this isn't an easy question. Because the calendar year is 365 days long (366 in leap years), it doesn't divide evenly by the seven days of the week.

Also, the Earth goes around the Sun in about 365-1/4 days, so a calendar tends to drift over time. That's why the same date falls on different weekdays in different years.

This is made even more complicated by a change in calendars that took place in 1582. Our modern calendar has its roots in ancient Rome, in a calendar reform conducted by Julius Caesar. Caesar commissioned mathematicians to attack the problem, and they came up with the idea of leap years, and thus standardized the calendar for centuries to come. This was called the Julian calendar.

Over time, however, the small errors in Caesar's calculation compounded. That's why Pope Gregory XIII commissioned the Gregorian calendar, used in most of the world today. Some countries converted in 1582, when the calendar was first developed; some converted later; other still haven't changed.

Gregorian and Julian aren't the only types of calendars. The Hebrew year, the Islamic year, and many other calendars are used in different parts of the world and among different people.

You can convert Gregorian dates to other calendars, including the Hebrew calendar, the Islamic calendar, and even the Mayan calendar by visiting the Fourmilab Calendar Converter at http://www.fourmilab.ch/documents/calendar/.

Chinese calendar systems are quite complex and have changed several times; a full discussion is far beyond the scope of this book. If you're interested, you can find information here: http://www.hermetic.ch/cal_stud/chinese_cal.htm.

On Names and Dates

Historians use "CE" (Common Era) and "BCE" (Before the Common Era) instead of the more common "AD" (Anno Domini, or Year of Our Lord) and "BC" (Before Christ), reflecting the fact that the year-numbering system established by the Gregorian calendar is used throughout the world in many countries not culturally Christian.

The CE/BCE designation dates back to at least 1708, and has been adopted as a standard by the United Nations and the Universal Postal Union. Because this series of books covers events and people of all nations and cultures, we use the CE/BCE terms.

The abbreviation "O.S." ("Old Style") on some dates refers to the fact that the Russian Empire did not switch from the Julian to the Gregorian calendar at the same time as the rest of Europe, and therefore some figures and events have two dates.

Also, in the Julian calendar in England in the 16th century, the year began on March 25 rather than January 1. To avoid confusion with Gregorian dates, dates between January and March were often written using both years.

People and events whose original names are not in the Western alphabet have their native names (where possible) in the appropriate script shown in parenthesis. If you are using an e-reader to access an electronic version of this book, all characters don't always display on all devices.

A 50-year brass perpetual calendar.

Quote of the Day

"Time is an illusion, lunchtime doubly so."

Douglas Adams,
from *The Hitchhiker's Guide to the Galaxy*

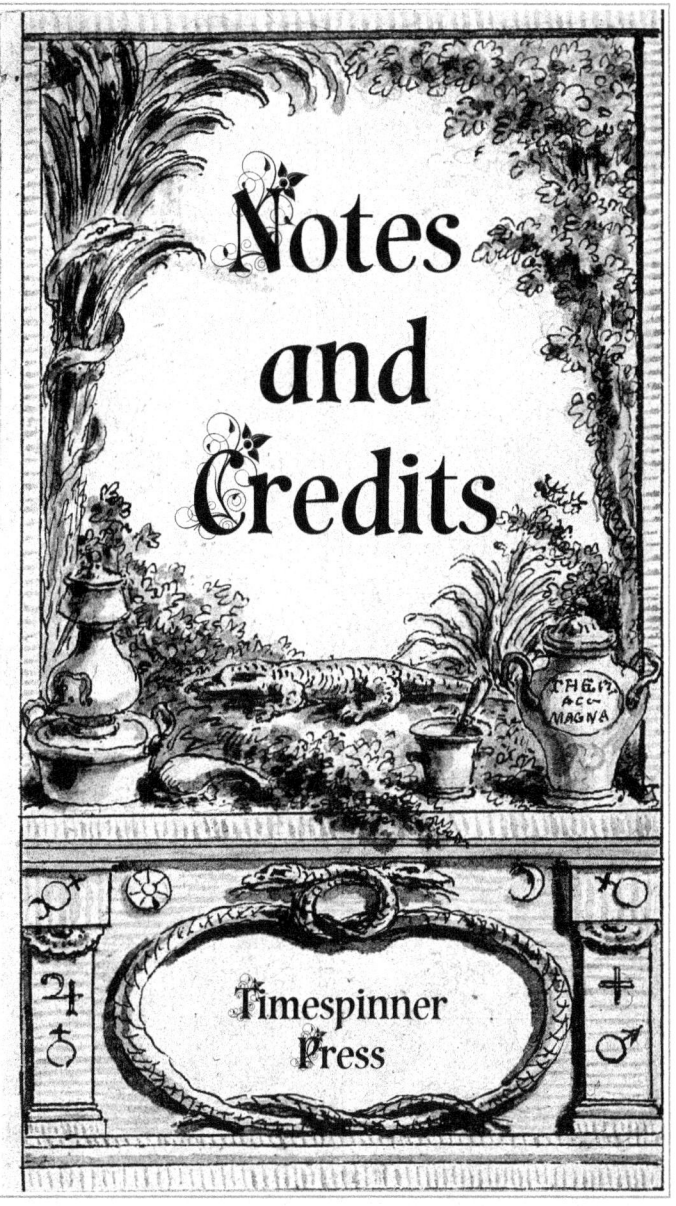

Notes
and
Credits

CHEM
ACC
MAGNA

Timespinner
Press

Cartoon by John T. McCutcheon

Copyright, Credit, and Contact

Follow Us

Our blog "This Day in History" (http://
timespinnerpress.com/this-day-in-history/) features short
articles on events and people associated with each day, and
updates several times each week. Also subscribe to the
"Quote of the Day" at http://timespinnerpress.com/quote-
of-the-day/. You can get daily links by following us on
Facebook at TimespinnerPress, or on Twitter as
@sidewisethinker.

Contact Us

Find an error or a format problem? Want information about
the series, about us, or about when the volume for your
special day might be available? Please email us at
editor@timespinnerpress.com. (We also take requests if your
special day isn't yet complete. Please give us at least six
weeks' notice if possible.)

Sources

We owe a great debt to Wikipedia, which is our first stop for
research. We attempt to make independent confirmation of
all important dates and facts through a variety of other
sources.

Other sources we frequently use include the Library of
Congress; "on this day" listings from *Encyclopedia Britannica*,
the *New York Times*, and the BBC; Omniglot for the names of
months in other languages; *Chase's Calendar of Events*; and, of
course, the always essential Google.

All art and photographs are either in the public domain, used under a Creative Commons license, or with a "fair use" justification, and most frequently come from Wikimedia Commons and the Library of Congress Prints and Photographs Division.

Attribution is provided where possible, or as requested by the copyright owner, or when there is particular historical significance, listed below. For information about any particular illustration or photograph, please contact us.

Credits

1. The cover photograph of New Year's Eve fireworks in Niederau, Tyrol, Austria, was taken on January 1, 2013 by "Ximeg," and uploaded to Wikimedia Commons. It is used here under CC BY-SA 3.0.

2. The illustration of the month of January used on the back cover is from the French Gothic illuminated manuscript *Les Très Riches Heures du duc de Berry* by the Limbourg Brothers, Jean Colombe, and an intermediate painter whose name is lost to history.

3. The box graphic used on the first page is from a 1916 pamphlet entitled "Divorce versus Democracy" authored by G. K. Chesterton, originally published in London by the Society of St. Peter and St. Paul. It is in the public domain in the US because it was published prior to 1923, and is in the public domain in all countries (including the country of origin) in which the copyright time is the author's life plus 70 years or less.

4. The graphic design for the section pages in this book is from a design originally created for a pharmacy label. It is from Wellcome Images (ICV No 11073, photo V0010813), and is used here under CC BY-SA 4.0.

5. The 1910 New Year's Day postcard was originally copyrighted by John Winsch in 1910. It is in the public domain because its copyright has expired.

6. The 1910 Happy New Year postcard is by Frances Brundage; it is in the public domain because its copyright has expired.

7. The French postcard *Bonne année fêtée au champagne* is in the public domain because its copyright has expired and its author is unknown. The 1922 illustration of Father Time is from the book *Slings and Arrows* by Edwin Francis Edgett (Boston: B. J. Brimmer). It is in the public domain because its copyright has expired.

8. The photograph of an Italian immigrant at Ellis Island was taken by Lewis Wicks Hine, and is from the collection of the Los Angeles County Museum of Art (accession number M. 90.30.2). It is in the public domain because its copyright has expired.

9. The 1864 painting "First Reading of the Emancipation Proclamation by Abraham Lincoln" is by Francis Bicknell Carpenter, and can be found in the west staircase of the Senate Wing of the US Capitol. It is in the public domain because its copyright has expired.

10. The photograph of the US federal penitentiary on Alcatraz Island is by Jon Sullivan, who released the image into the public domain.

11. The 2005 photograph of the Euro neon sign was taken by Lar Aronsson and is used here under CC BY-SA 1.0.

12. The 1768 portrait of Paul Revere by John Singleton Copley is from the collection of the Museum of Fine Arts, Boston (accession number 30.781). It is in the public domain because its copyright has expired.

13. The 1886 self-portrait of Alfred Stieglitz is in the public domain because its copyright has expired.

14. The 1961 photograph of J. Edgar Hoover was taken by Marion S. Trikoso for *US News and World Report*. It is part of the *US News and World Report* collection at the Library of Congress (digital ID ppmsc.03262). Per the deed of gift, all rights in these photographs have been dedicated to the public.

15. The painting of Betsy Ross sewing the American flag is by Jean Leon Gerome Ferris, from the series *The Pageant of a Nation*, and is in the public domain because its copyright has expired. The image is courtesy of the Library of Congress, digital ID cph.3g09905.

16. The 1944 photograph of Xavier Cugat appeared in an advertisement in the *Billboard 1944 Music Yearbook*. It is in the

public domain because it was first published in the United States between 1923 and 1963 without a copyright notice.

17. The 1930 publicity photograph of Matthew Beard from *School's Out* is in the public domain because it was first published in the United States between 1923 and 1963, and although there may or may not have been an original copyright notice, the copyright was not renewed. Traditionally, publicity photographs are not copyrighted because of the way in which they are intended to be used.

18. The 1901 photograph of Gustave Whitehead with his monoplane is in the public domain because its copyright has expired. The photographer is unknown.

19. The 1934 Goudey baseball card of Henry "Hank" Greenberg is in the public domain because it was first published in the United States between 1923 and 1963, and although there may or may not have been an original copyright notice, the copyright was not renewed.

20. The 1948 MGM publicity photograph of Hank Williams is in the public domain because it was first published in the United States between 1923 and 1963, and without a copyright notice. Traditionally, publicity photographs are not copyrighted because of the way in which they are intended to be used.

21. The 1959 publicity photograph of Maurice Chevalier is in the public domain because it was first published in the United States between 1923 and 1963, and without a copyright notice. Traditionally, publicity photographs are not copyrighted because of the way in which they are intended to be used.

22. The photograph of Grace Hopper at the UNIVAC keyboard was taken around 1960, and is in the collection of the Smithsonian Institution (83-14878). It is used here under CC-BY-SA 2.0.

23. The 1932 photograph of Helen Wills was taken by *Agence de presse Meurisse* and is from the collection of the *Bibliothèque nationale de France*. It is in the public domain in France, its country of origin, and in other countries where the copyright term is the author's life plus 70 years or less.

24. The photograph of a Kwanzaa ritual was taken by Christopher Myers, a US Air Force airman or employee, as

part of that person's official duties, and is therefore in the public domain.

25. The song poster for "The Twelve Days of Christmas" was created in 2012 by Xavier Romero-Frias, and is used here under CC BY-SA 3.0.

26. The 2016 photograph of a bloody mary cocktail is by "Tibuhero" and is used here under CC BY-SA 4.0.

27. The photograph of a person reading a braille book was taken by Antonio X. Alonso in 2009. It is used here under CC BY-SA 2.0.

28. The 1896 postcard "January" by Eugène Grasset is in the public domain because its copyright has expired.

29. The 1815 woodcut of a Regency era wedding proposal is in the public domain because its copyright has expired.

30. The painting *January* is from the *Brevarium Gremani*, circa 1510, and is in the public domain because its copyright has expired.

31. The graphic of "Why" in several languages was created in 2011 by "Maierstrahl," and is used here under CC BY-SA 3.0.

32. The 1968 USSR postage stamp "Prospecting Geologist with Found Diamond and Red Crystals-Pyropes (Garnets)" is not an object of copyright according to Part IV of Civil Code No. 230-FZ of the Russian Federation (2006).

33. The 1886 painting "Vase with Red and White Carnations on a Yellow Background" by Vincent Van Gogh is in the public domain because its copyright has expired.

34. The German New Year's greeting card was made circa 1900. It is in the public domain because its copyright has expired.

35. The 2006 photograph of a red plum blossom (*prunus mume*) was taken by Frank Gualtieri, who released the photograph into the public domain.

36. The illustration of camellias by Clara Maria Pope is from Samuel Curtis' *Monograph on the Genus Camellia*, published in 1819. It is in the public domain because its copyright has expired.

37. The celestial sphere is from *Scenography of the Ptolemaic Cosmography*, by Johannes van Loon, based on Andreas Cellarius's *Harmonia Macrocosmica*, 1660. It is in the public domain because its copyright has expired.

38. The 1906 automobile calendar is by Edward Penfield, and is in the collection of the Library of Congress Prints and Photographs Division. It is in the public domain because its copyright has expired.

39. The 50-year perpetual calendar photograph is in the public domain.

40. The cartoon by John T. McCutcheon is from his 1905 collection *The Mysterious Stranger and Other Cartoons by John T. McCutcheon*. It is in the public domain because its copyright has expired.

41. The painting "January" is from the calendar book *Festkalender* by Hans Thoma. It is in the pubic domain because its copyright has expired.

License Description and Terms

Aside from material purely in the public domain, photographs and other material in this book are used under specific licenses permitting free use, usually with an attribution requirement. For full text and terms of these licenses, click or enter the appropriate links below. If you believe there is an error in the copyright status or attribution of any of these images, please email us.

- Creative Commons Attribution 2.0 Generic (CC-BY 2.0): http://creativecommons.org/licenses/by/2.0/deed.en
- Creative Commons Attribution-Share Alike 3.0 Generic (CC-BY-SA 3.0): http://creativecommons.org/licenses/by-sa/3.0/
- Creative Commons Attribution-Share Alike 2.5 Generic (CC-BY-SA 2.5): http://creativecommons.org/licenses/by-sa/2.5/deed.en
- Creative Commons Attribution-Share Alike 2.0 Generic (CC-BY-SA 2.0): http://creativecommons.org/licenses/by/2.0/deed.en
- Creative Commons Attribution-Share Alike 1.0 Generic (CC-BY-SA 1.0): http://creativecommons.org/licenses/by-sa/1.0/deed.en

- CC0 1.0 Universal (CC0 1.0) Public Domain Dedication (CC0 1.0) http://creativecommons.org/publicdomain/zero/1.0/deed.en

- GNU Free Documentation License (GFDL): http://en.wikipedia.org/wiki/Wikipedia:Text_of_the_GNU_Free_Documentation_License

- License Art Libre (Free Art License): http://artlibre.org

Timespinner
Press

January, by Hans Thoma

Other Books from Timespinner Press

The Story of a Special Day
Michael Dobson

A series of (eventually) 366 volumes covering everything that happened on your special day! Events, births, deaths, quotes, holidays, and much more. It's like a birthday card they'll never throw away!

US$7.95 print / US$2.99 ebook.

From Plassey to Pakistan
Humayun Mirza

The history of British Colonial India and the formation of Pakistan from the unique perspective of the son of Pakistan's first president and last of the royal line of Bengal, Bihar, and Orissa! This unique historical document tells the inside story of this distinguished family, including the detailed story of the coup that toppled his father from power!

US$27.95 print

A Whole New Navy: America's War in the Pacific

Miles Durr

The most comprehensive and detailed description of America's naval war in the Pacific ever—every battle, every ship, every task force and every task group from Pearl Harbor through the Japanese surrender! A must-have for the collection of every World War II buff!

US$29.95 print

Improbable History: The Weird, the Obscure, and the Strangely Important

edited by Michael Dobson

From the birth of Western civilization to the rescue of Apollo 13, from the Leaning Tower of Pisa to Florence's Duomo, history has often turned on small, improbable details. Whatever happened to the ancient Samaritan people? Why did a fortuitous rainstorm allow the British to conquer India? How did an air raid in Italy lead to the development of chemotherapy? What happened when Albert Einstein met Adolf Hitler on the streets of Berlin? How did the Japanese manage to attack the US mainland using balloons? A cast of award-winning writers tackle some of the strangest tales in history!

US$19.95 print